Super Spiders

Charlotte Guillain

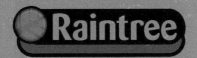

Chicago, Illinois

© 2013 Raintree
an imprint of Capstone Global Library, LLC
Chicago, Illinois

Edited by Daniel Nunn, Rebecca Rissman, and Catherine Veitch
Designed by Victoria Allen
Picture research by Mica Brancic
Production by Victoria Fitzgerald
Originated by Capstone Global Library Ltd

Library of Congress Cataloging-in-Publication Data
Guillain, Charlotte.
  Super spiders / Charlotte Guillain.
     pages. cm.—(Walk on the wild side)
  Includes bibliographical references and index.
  ISBN 978-1-4109-5219-6 (hb)
  ISBN 978-1-4109-5226-4 (pb)
  1. Spiders—Juvenile literature. I. Title.
  QL452.2.G85 2013
  595.4'4—dc23   2012034701

Image Credits
Alamy: cbstockfoto, 5; Getty Images: Steve Satushek, 4, TacioPhilip, 20, Uwe-Bergwitz, 19; Nature Picture Library: Alex Hyde, 10, 17, Amy Johansson, 29, Bernard Castelein, 18, Ingo Arndt, 15, 28, Kim Taylor, 8, 24, Meul/ARCO, 26, Nick Garbutt, 9, Premaphotos/Preston-Mafham, 12, Stephen Dalton, 7, 11, 14, 25, Wegner/ARCO, 21; Shutterstock: Aleksandr Kurganov, 16, Eric Isselée, cover, Jarp2, 22, kurt_G, 27, Michal Ninger, 23, MilanB, 13, Yongsan, 6

We would like to thank Michael Bright for his invaluable help in the preparation of this book.

Every effort has been made to contact copyright holders of material reproduced in this book. Any omissions will be rectified in subsequent printings if notice is given to the publisher.

All the Internet addresses (URLs) given in this book were valid at the time of going to press. However, due to the dynamic nature of the Internet, some addresses may have changed, or sites may have changed or ceased to exist since publication. While the author and publisher regret any inconvenience this may cause readers, no responsibility for any such changes can be accepted by either the author or the publisher.

Some words are shown in bold, **like this**. You can find out what they mean by looking in the glossary.

Contents

Introducing Spiders

How do you feel when you see spiders? Lots of people run away from them! But spiders are amazing and helpful creatures. They eat many insects that bite humans or spread diseases.

Are you afraid of spiders, or do you find them interesting?

garden spider

redback
spider

Did you know?

Only a few spiders bite humans and harm them. The redback spider is one of them!

Where Do Spiders Live?

Spiders live in many different **habitats**. They can live in gardens, forests, fields, deserts, and swamps. There might be spiders living in webs in the corners of your home.

jumping spider

Spiders will live wherever there is food for them to catch.

Did you know?

Water spiders make a little air-filled hiding place underwater. They wait inside for **prey** to swim past!

What Do Spiders Look Like?

Spiders have eight legs. Spiders' bodies have two sections. The **cephalothorax** is the spider's head and middle section. The **abdomen** is the lower part of the spider's body.

tarantula spider

cephalothorax

abdomen

Did you know?
The hairs on a spider's legs help it to move over its sticky web without getting stuck.

weaver spider

Super Senses

Most spiders have four pairs of eyes. Spiders that build webs do not have very good eyesight, but hunting spiders see well. They use their eyes to see their **prey.**

jumping spider

tarantula
spider

Did you know?

Spiders have fine hairs on their legs that they use to feel **vibrations** when prey is moving nearby.

Cunning Camouflage

Many spiders are **camouflaged** to hide them from **prey** and from **predators** such as birds. This spider uses camouflage to hide in a yellow flower that many insects visit.

crab spider

Garden spiders have patchy, blotchy coloring. This makes it hard for birds to see them.

Spinning Silk

All spiders can spin **silk**. Most spiders have **spinnerets** on their **abdomen**, where the silk is spun. All spiders leave a silk thread called a dragline behind them. They use it to lower themselves from high places or to escape from danger.

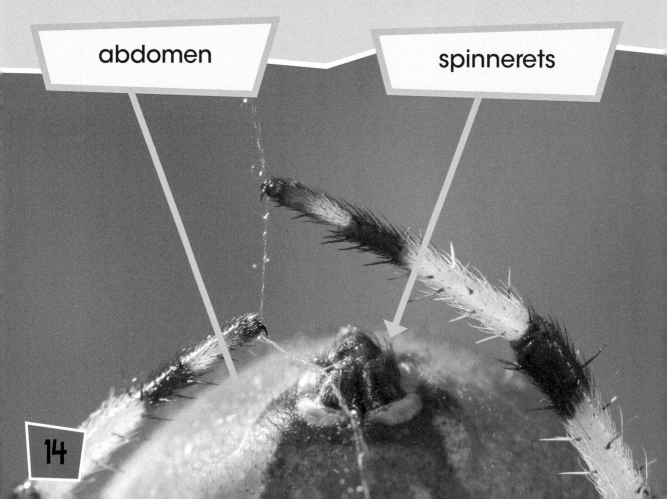

abdomen

spinnerets

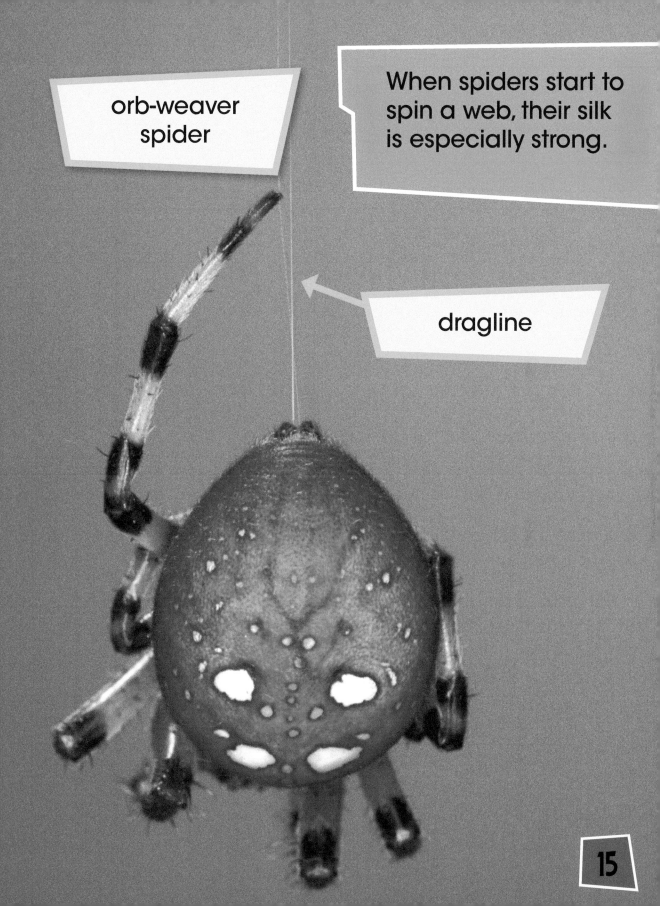

orb-weaver spider

When spiders start to spin a web, their silk is especially strong.

dragline

Spinning Webs

Some spiders spin webs out of **silk** to catch food. Many spiders build orb webs, with lines of silk covered with a spiral of sticky thread. Other spiders spin tubes out of silk, called funnel webs. They hide inside and wait for insects to walk into the tube.

orb-web spider

orb web

funnel web

labyrinth
spider

17

Catching Prey

Orb-web-weaving spiders lie in wait in the center of their webs. When an insect gets stuck on the web, the spider feels the **vibrations** and moves in to kill the **prey**.

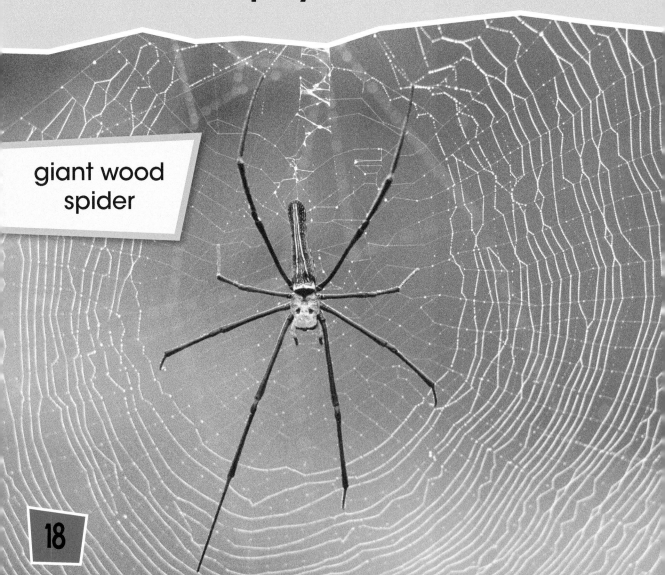

giant wood spider

tarantula spider

Did you know?

Hunting spiders do not build webs. They lie in wait for prey and ambush, or surprise, it.

Fierce Fangs

All spiders bite their **prey** with fangs, which are long, pointed teeth. Most squirt **venom** into their victims to kill or **paralyze** them so they cannot escape. The most poisonous spider in the world is the Brazilian wandering spider.

Brazilian wandering spider

Did you know?

Luckily, most spiders do not usually bite humans. Doctors have made medicines to help people who do get bitten.

tarantula spider

fangs

Digesting Dinner

After a spider has caught an insect in its web and injected it with **venom**, it will often wrap the **prey** up in **silk** thread. When the prey is wrapped in silk, the spider injects it with digestive juices. These juices turn the prey to liquid, which the spider then sucks up.

orb-web
spider

four-spot
orb-weaver
spider

Recycling

Many spiders eat their web and any small bugs that have stuck to it after they have finished with it. Spiders can **recycle** the **silk** thread they eat in their bodies and use it to make a new web.

spiked spider

wasp spider

Did you know?

Some spiders make repairs to a web and use it more than once.

Baby Spiders

When most female spiders lay eggs, they wrap them in **silk** to protect them. Some spiders, such as the garden spider, die before their eggs hatch. Baby spiders are called spiderlings. They stay inside the silk case until it is warm enough to come out.

Nursery web spiders guard their eggs before they hatch.

Wolf spiders carry their eggs and spiderlings.

27

Life for a Spider

Spiders survive all over the world, except in Antarctica. They are all **predators**, and some produce deadly **venom** that is harmful to much bigger animals. But spiders are also amazing! They can weave beautiful webs and help to get rid of many insects that are pests for humans.

Black widow spiders are famous for their venomous bite.

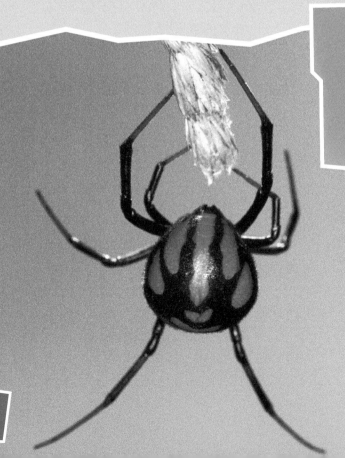

orb-web
spider

Did you know?

Spiders are not insects.
They belong to a group
called **arachnids**.

Glossary

abdomen lower part of a spider's body

arachnid group of creatures with a body in two parts and four pairs of legs

camouflage coloring or disguise that hides an animal from view

cephalothorax spider's head and middle section

habitat natural home for an animal

paralyze stop something from moving

predator animal that kills and eats other animals

prey animal killed by another animal for food

recycle use again

silk thread produced by a spider

spinneret openings on a spider's body that make silk

venom poison

vibration shaking movement

Find Out More

Books

Gilpin, Rebecca. *Spiders* (Usborne Beginners). Tulsa, Okla.: EDC, 2007.

Hartley, Karen. *Spider* (Bug Books). Chicago: Heinemann Library, 2008.

Morgan, Sally. *Spiders* (Amazing Animal Hunters). Mankato, Minn.: Amicus, 2011.

Thomas, Isabel. *Scorpion vs. Tarantula* (Animals Head to Head). Chicago: Raintree, 2006.

Web sites

Facthound offers a safe, fun way to find web sites related to this book. All the sites on Facthound have been researched by our staff.

Here's all you do:
Visit **www.facthound.com**
Type in this code: 9781410952196

Index